Genre Persuasive Article

Essential Question

Why are rules important?

Do People Need RULES?

by Anton Wilson

Chapter 1

Rules Protect Us

The government makes rules carefully.

Do we need **rules**? Parents make rules for a family. Schools make rules for students. Our government makes rules, too.

Rules are important. Rules help keep us safe. They help us get along with each other.

A geyser at Yellowstone National Park

National Parks Need Rules

National Parks are **public** places. Anyone can visit. Yellowstone was the first national park. Visitors must follow the rules. Rules protect our national parks.

This park is in Tennessee and North Carolina.

The United States has more than 400 national parks. Rules protect these places.

STOP AND CHECK

Why do national parks need rules?

Chapter 2

Food Rules

This stamp tells you the meat was checked.

We Need Food Rules

Food rules help keep our food safe. The government checks some foods. If these foods are safe, they get a stamp.

Food rules keep school lunches safe.

School Lunches

Schools follow rules about food. They **serve** food that was checked by the government. That way students have safe food.

Rules tell people how to cook meat safely.

Food Safety

Food safety rules are important. You can eat a **raw** apple. But some raw foods can make you sick. Rules tell people how to cook food safely.

STOP AND CHECK

Why are food safety rules important?

Image Source/Getty Images

How can I safely store eggs?

Type of Egg	Refrigerator	Freezer
raw eggs in shell	Refrigerate raw eggs for 3 to 5 weeks.	Do not freeze raw eggs in their shells.
raw egg whites	Refrigerate raw egg whites for 2 to 4 days.	Freeze raw egg whites for 12 months.
hard-cooked eggs	Refrigerate hard-cooked eggs for 1 week.	Do not freeze hard-cooked eggs.

The government tells us how to store food. Look at the chart above. It shows rules about how long to keep eggs. Food rules help keep us safe.

These people learn how to take their medicine.

Medicines

Rules for **medicines** are important. The government tests medicines for safety. Then the government may approve a medicine. Stores can sell the approved medicine.

STOP AND CHECK

Why does the government make sure medicines are tested?

Chapter 3

Animal Rules

There are rules for fishing.

Why do we need animal rules? The rules help protect animals. The government has rules about hunting and fishing. That way animals are not hunted too much.

Photodisc Collection/Getty Images

Rules protect animals that live in the wild.

Government rules also protect the places where animals live. People can visit these places. But they must follow the rules.

STOP AND CHECK

How do government rules protect animals?

Illustration: Rob Schuster

Chapter 4

Idea Rules

There is a copyright page at the front of a book.

Some government rules protect ideas. Certain rules say that people cannot **copy** the ideas in a book. These rules help **writers** protect their work.

Andersen Ross/Photodisc/Getty Images

The TM on the box stands for "trademark." No one else can use this cereal name.

Rules Protect Inventors

Inventors get a patent to protect their ideas. A patent is a paper that says the inventor came up with the idea first.

Rules protect the patents of things in your home.

This rule protects people with good ideas.

People need government rules. The world is a better place when we follow the rules.

STOP AND CHECK

Why do we need rules to protect ideas?

Respond to Reading

Summarize

Summarize *Do People Need Rules?* The chart may help you.

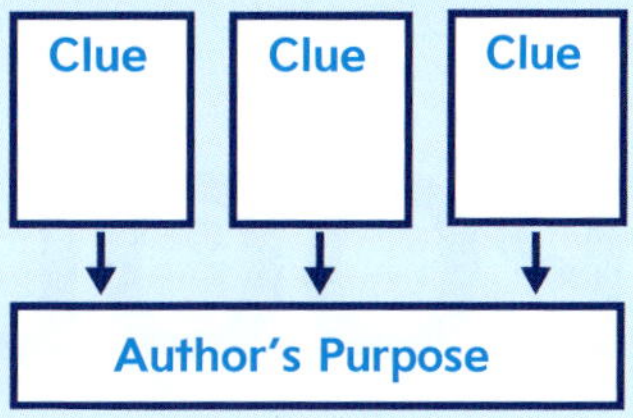

Text Evidence

1. What is the author's purpose in Chapter 2? **Author's Purpose**
2. What do inventors get to help them protect their work? **Vocabulary**
3. Write about why the author feels that rules are important. **Write About Reading**

Genre Persuasive Article

Compare Texts

Read about why pool rules are important.

POOL RULES

Swimming is fun if you stay safe. Pools show their rules on signs. That way everyone can see them.

Many places have public pools.

Enigma/Alamy Stock Photo

No Diving

Some pools are deep, and others are shallow. You cannot dive into shallow water. You might hit your head.

No Running

The area around a pool is wet and slippery. You should walk, not run, near pools.

No Eating or Drinking

You cannot have food or drinks in the pool. The water could get dirty. Glass bottles might break. People could cut their feet.

Follow the pool rules. You will stay safe and have fun!

Make Connections

How do pool rules protect you?
Essential Question

How are government rules and pool rules alike? Text to Text

Focus on

Social Studies

Purpose To find out why classroom rules are important

What to Do

Step 1 Work with a partner. Write down two classroom rules.

Step 2 Write down how each rule helps your class. Use a chart like this.

Rule	How It Helps

Step 3 Compare your chart with another group.